Cockroaches

Cockroaches

Patrick Merrick

THE CHILD'S WORLD®

Published in the United States of America by The Child's World®
PO Box 326
Chanhassen, MN 55317-0326
800-599-READ
www.childsworld.com

Project Manager Mary Berendes
Editor Katherine Stevenson, Ph.D.
Designer Mary Berendes
**Our sincere thanks to Robert Mitchell, Ph.D.,
for his input and guidance on this book.**

Photo Credits
ANIMALS ANIMALS © David M. Dennis: 30
ANIMALS ANIMALS © Jack Clark: 9
ANIMALS ANIMALS © John Pontier: 20
ANIMALS ANIMALS © Michael Dick: 2
ANIMALS ANIMALS © OSF/Marty Cordano: 15 (top)
ANIMALS ANIMALS © Patti Murray: 23
ANIMALS ANIMALS © Raymond Mendez: 15 (bottom), 16
© Catrina Genovese/Index Stock Imagery, Inc.: 6
© Robert & Linda Mitchell: cover, 10, 13, 19, 24, 26
© Robert Pickett/CORBIS: 29

Library of Congress Cataloging-in-Publication Data
Merrick, Patrick.
Cockroaches / by Patrick Merrick.
p. cm. — (Naturebooks series)
Summary: Describes the physical characteristics, behavior,
habitat, and life cycle of cockroaches.
ISBN 1-56766-206-4 (lib. bdg. : alk. paper)
1. Cockroaches—Juvenile literature. [1. Cockroaches.] I. Title.
II. Series: Naturebooks (Chanhassen, Minn.)
QL505.5 .M47 2003
595.7'28—dc21
2002151471

$17.95

J
595.728
MER
c. 1

On the cover...

Front cover: From close up, you can see the details on this American cockroach's body.
Page 2: This tree stump is covered with Madagascar hissing cockroaches.

Table of Contents

The sun has gone down, and everyone in the house is getting ready for bed. The lights go off, and soon everyone is asleep. In a dark corner of the kitchen, a tiny creature crawls out of a cupboard. Soon another appears, and then another. The little creatures scurry across the floor, searching for food. What are these nighttime visitors? They're cockroaches!

← This giant Peruvian cockroach is feeding on food scraps at night.

What Are Cockroaches?

Cockroaches are part of a group of animals called **insects**. Most insects have two sets of wings and six legs. The body of an adult insect is divided into three different areas. The front area is the head. The middle area is the **thorax**, or chest. The back area is the **abdomen**, or stomach region.

Cockroaches are one of the oldest and most basic of all insects. In fact, cockroaches have lived on Earth for over 350 million years! In all that time, they have changed very little. Ancient cockroaches looked and acted a lot like modern ones.

Here you can see the body parts of this ⇒
smoky brown cockroach.

A cockroach has no bones in its body. Instead, it has a hard shell, or **exoskeleton**. The exoskeleton is covered with wax that makes the cockroach waterproof. Cockroaches can swim in pipes and stay underwater for a long time.

Cockroaches are perfectly designed for hiding and escaping. Their flat, oval bodies can squeeze into small cracks. In fact, an adult cockroach can fit into a crack no thicker than a coin!

⇐ The exoskeleton of this orangehead roach is shiny from the roach's own wax.

Cockroaches have two sets of wings and six strong legs. The legs are covered with hard hairs. Each leg ends in a pair of claws instead of a foot. The hairs and claws allow the cockroach to cling to almost anything.

A cockroach's feelers, or **antennae**, are longer than its body. The cockroach uses its antennae to taste, feel, smell, and find its way around. The cockroach's eyes and mouth are on its head. Even after losing its head, a cockroach can live for over a week!

This American cockroach is crawling across a floor in ⇒ southern Arizona. You can see the hairs on its legs.

Are There Different Kinds of Cockroaches?

There are about 4,000 different types, or **species**, of cockroaches living around the world. Scientists think there might be many more species just waiting to be found.

Most cockroaches in the United States are brown or black. They are about one-half to two inches long. Cockroaches in hotter **tropical** areas are more colorful. Some are red, green, or even yellow. These tropical cockroaches are also much bigger. The *Madagascar hissing cockroach* is over four inches long! When it gets scared, it hisses like a snake.

Top: These Madagascar hissing ⇒
cockroaches are resting on a leaf.

Bottom: This giant cockroach is crawling
on a person's hand in Trinidad.

Where Do Cockroaches Like to Live?

Cockroaches can live almost anywhere, even in places that are fairly cold or dry. But they especially like hot, damp areas with good hiding places and lots of food to eat. We think of cockroaches as living in cities, but most cockroach species live in rain forests where people never see them. Only a few species live around people.

⇐ These adult and young Asian cockroaches are crawling on a forest floor in Florida.

What Do Cockroaches Eat?

Cockroaches are **nocturnal**, which means that they rest all day and come out at night to eat. They love to live in kitchens, restaurants, and offices. When it gets dark and the people leave, the cockroaches help themselves to leftover food.

If cockroaches can't find any food before the sun comes up, they go hungry. They can live for weeks without food. Hunger is rarely a problem, though, because cockroaches will eat anything! They eat meat, garbage, plants, paper, glue, and even animal waste. Special feelers called *palps* on their mouths check the food first to make sure it is safe.

You can clearly see the two pairs of ⇒ palps on this death's head cockroach.

After mating with a male only once, a female cockroach can produce eggs for the rest of her life. She lays a *sac* of eggs and puts it in a hiding place. In a few weeks, up to 40 baby cockroaches hatch from their eggs and break out of the protective sac.

⇐ *Top*: This is what a cockroach egg sac looks like from the outside.

Bottom: When the sac is opened, you can see the baby cockroaches inside.

A baby cockroach looks like a small adult cockroach except that it is white and has no wings. Because of its hard, shell-like skin, the young cockroach cannot grow the way people do. When it gets too big for its skin, it simply sheds the skin, or **molts**. A new, bigger skin lies underneath.

Cockroaches molt six to 12 times while growing into adults. If a young cockroach loses a leg or an antenna, it can grow a new one! The new body part appears the next time the cockroach molts.

This cockroach is shedding its skin in a Malaysian ⇒ cave. Its new skin has not yet turned brown.

Adult cockroaches are hard to catch, but even so, they have many enemies. Spiders, mice, frogs, lizards, and other small animals eat cockroaches. Some wasps lay their eggs in cockroach egg sacs. When the wasp eggs hatch, the baby wasps eat the cockroach eggs for their first meal!

⇐ Here you can see a female Madagascar hissing cockroach and her young. Young cockroaches are in more danger of being eaten by enemies than adults are.

Cockroaches are good at escaping because they can detect very tiny movements. Humans use their eyes to see things move. Cockroaches, however, can feel movements with their legs! Each leg has three knees that can feel the movements of other insects. Cockroaches also have two special spikes, called *cerci*. These spikes help the cockroach feel if anything is sneaking up on it.

Cockroaches' biggest enemy is people. Most people dislike cockroaches and try to kill any they see.

⇐ You can see the cerci on the underside of this death's head cockroach.

Are Cockroaches Pests?

Cockroaches have many habits that do not fit well with living around people. They crawl around rotten food and animal waste and then walk over and begin eating the people's food. They also have a bad smell and leave their droppings everywhere. Many scientists believe that cockroaches can carry diseases.

Cockroaches can cause other health problems, too. Being around cockroaches gives some people a skin rash or makes it hard for them to breathe.

This common cockroach is crawling on a ⇒
plate of food that was left out overnight.

How Can You Get Rid of Cockroaches?

Once cockroaches enter a building, they are hard to get out. Many people hire someone to come in and spray poisons that kill the cockroaches. Filling cracks and holes where the cockroaches hide is important, too. It's also a good idea to clean up food and crumbs and to stop any water drips or leaks.

Cockroaches are very good at living in almost any situation. In fact, they are one of nature's oldest and most interesting survivors!

⇐ This American cockroach is feeding on
a sandwich that was not cleaned up.

Glossary

abdomen (AB-doh-men)
An animal's stomach area is called its abdomen. Cockroaches and other insects have an abdomen.

antennae (an-TEN-nee)
Many insects have long feelers, called antennae, that sense the things around them. Cockroaches have very long antennae.

exoskeleton (eks-oh-SKELL-eh-ton)
Instead of skin, many insects have a hard covering called an exoskeleton. Cockroaches have an exoskeleton.

insects (IN-sekt)
Insects are animals with six legs and a body that is divided into three areas. Cockroaches are insects.

molt (MOLT)
When an animal molts, it sheds its outer layer of skin, fur, or feathers. Young cockroaches molt as they grow bigger.

nocturnal (nok-TUR-null)
Animals that are nocturnal are active at night and rest during the day. Cockroaches are nocturnal.

species (SPEE-sheez)
A species is a separate type of an animal. There are at least 4,000 species of cockroaches around the world.

thorax (THOR-ax)
The chest area of an insect is called its thorax. Cockroaches have a thorax.

tropical (TROP-ih-kull)
Tropical areas have hot, wet weather all year. Some large, colorful cockroaches live in tropical regions.

Index

Web Sites

Visit our homepage for lots of links about cockroaches!
http://www.childsworld.com/links.html

Note to Parents, Teachers, and Librarians:
We routinely verify our Web links to make sure they're safe, active sites—so encourage your readers to check them out!